The Metamorphosis to Freedom

The Metamorphosis to Freedom

ROBERT O. FISCH

Copyright © 2000
Written and illustrated by Robert O. Fisch
1st edition

ISBN 0-9679746-0-7
Library of Congress

All rights reserved. No part of this book may be reproduced in any form without the permission of Robert O. Fisch except for review purposes.

Minneapolis, MN

Printed in China

To my daughter, Rebecca Alexandria
May all young people be free some day

Contents

Historical Note	xi
Introduction: The Struggle for Freedom	xiii
My Youth in Budapest: The Threat to Freedom	2
In a Nazi Concentration Camp: The Loss of More than Freedom	6
Communism in Hungary: Freedom Postponed	10
The Revolution in Hungary: The Fight for Freedom	14
My Arrival in the United States: The Journey to Freedom	20
American Citizenship: Becoming Free	24
A New Life: Savoring Freedom	28
Fifty Years Later: A Free Man Visits the Past	34
A Lesson of Love: Treasuring Freedom	38
Epilogue: The Lesson of Freedom	42

I want to express my most sincere thanks to Norton Stillman,
who encouraged me to write this book and helped it become a reality,
and to Dr. Evan M. Maurer, who helped me share my thoughts with many.

Historical Note

- In Eastern Europe, the Danube River flows through Hungary and through its capital city, Budapest.

- Adolf Hitler became chancellor of Germany in 1933. He claimed absolute power, crushed all opposition to his Nazi Party and began the conquest of Europe that led to World War II. Nazi troops occupied Austria, Czechoslovakia, Poland, Denmark, Norway, Holland, Belgium and France. They attacked Yugoslavia, Greece and Russia, and indiscriminately bombarded England.

- At the same time, Hitler's SS storm troopers (the secret state police—the Gestapo) were carrying on a war against Jewish people in Europe. Jews were taken from their homes and sent to concentration camps, where many were tortured and killed. When the Nazis took over Hungary in 1944, they sent thousands of Jewish people to concentration camps every day.

- On D-day—June 6, 1944—Allied forces landed in France and began to turn the Nazis back. By the time the war ended, the Nazis had murdered six million Jews, including an estimated 800,000 Hungarians. These were not soldiers, but people who had been going about their daily business. This slaughter was the Holocaust.

- After the war, a new tyrant arose in Eastern Europe. The Soviet Union had been given control of Eastern Europe, which led to Communist dictatorships in Hungary and other countries. Hungarian students revolted against the Communists in 1956, but the brutal regime continued there until the breakup of the Soviet Union in 1989.

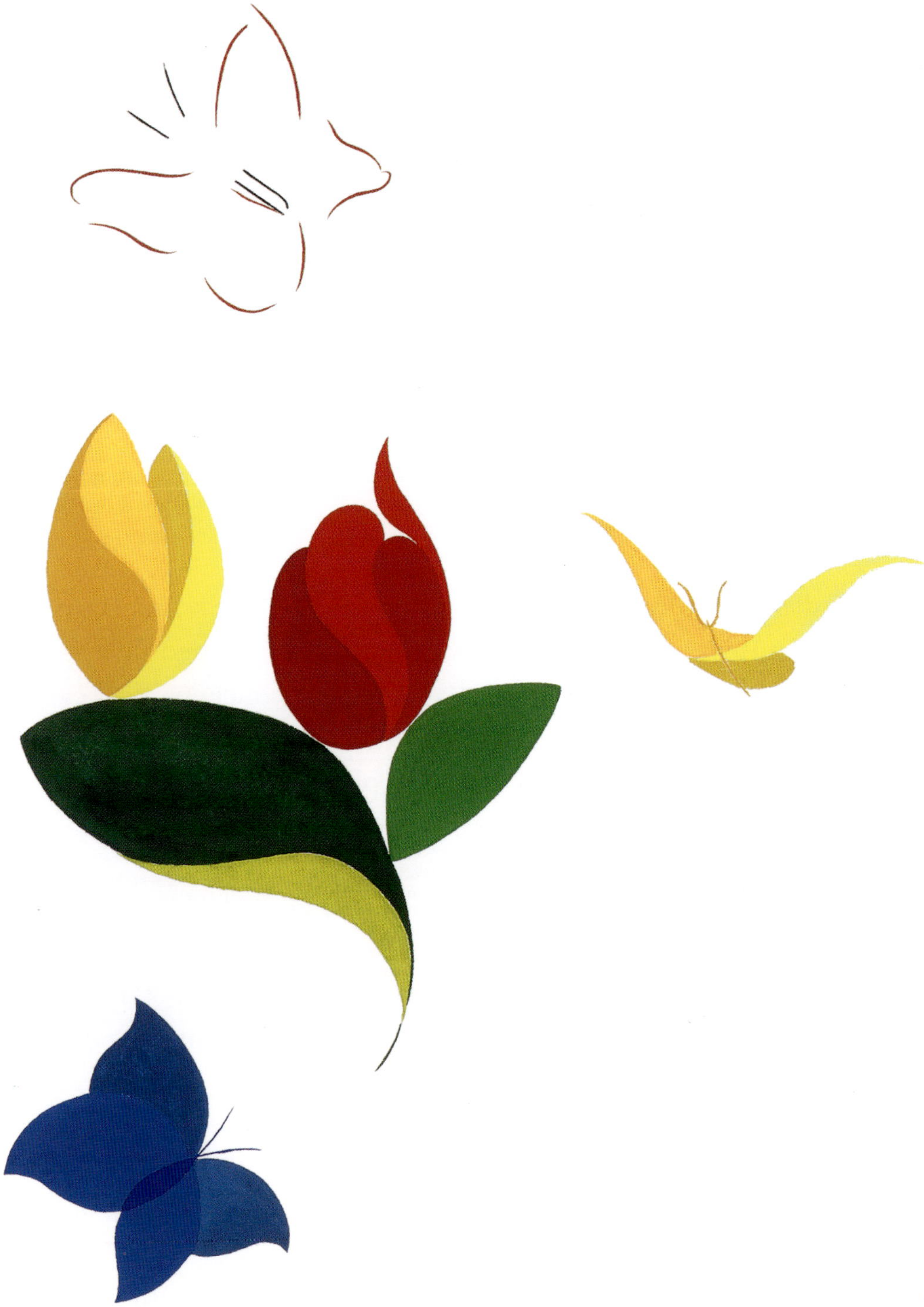

Introduction

The Struggle for Freedom

YOU ARE MOST LIKELY ONE OF THE FORTUNATE PEOPLE who were born in freedom. Only a fraction of people throughout history have been that lucky. I was not one of them.

When I was a young man in Hungary, the Nazis imprisoned, deported and killed Jewish people—including my father and many other members of my family—simply because they were Jews. Then the Communists took over my country and told me where and how I could practice medicine, for by then I had become a doctor.

I rebelled against the Communists, escaped from Hungary and eventually came to the United States.

I waited a long time for freedom, but it did not come when I expected it. There was no moment of celebration. Freedom came to me slowly, over many years.

Freedom did not accompany the long line of armored tanks that liberated me from a Nazi concentration camp. I did not find it when the people of Hungary rose up against the Russians who had taken over our country.

Nor was freedom waiting for me when I arrived in New York harbor on a U.S. Navy ship and first saw the Statue of Liberty. This was the beginning of a new life for me. I became an American citizen and received my first passport. I had never had a passport before because I was a refugee. My American passport opened the gates of countries that were previously closed to me, yet it did not make me free.

I assumed that liberation from oppression would make me free, but it was only the first step. Freedom does not come only from the outside. It is also a process that takes place within each person. It is like the metamorphosis of a caterpillar into a butterfly.

Freedom is independence, but it brings with it responsibilities as well as rights. It demands that we ask questions, make choices, take risks and accept consequences. If I had always followed the rules, I would have died more than once.

I was not born free. I sought freedom, and my journey to freedom was not an easy one. This makes it especially dear to me.

Some people do not choose freedom. Totalitarian governments provide a certain kind of security. People who live under dictatorships do not need to think for themselves. The government makes their decisions for them. In 1950 a Russian pilot received a considerable amount of money to desert and fly with his MIG 15 jet plane to the West. He came to the United States and lived in New York City, where nobody told him what to do, how to live, what to eat, how to dress. After six months he returned to Russia. He chose not to accept the challenges and responsibilities of being free.

Freedom is a struggle—and sometimes a lonely and difficult fight. When you achieve it, you feel like a climber reaching the summit of a mountain.

Be grateful for your freedom. Use it well.

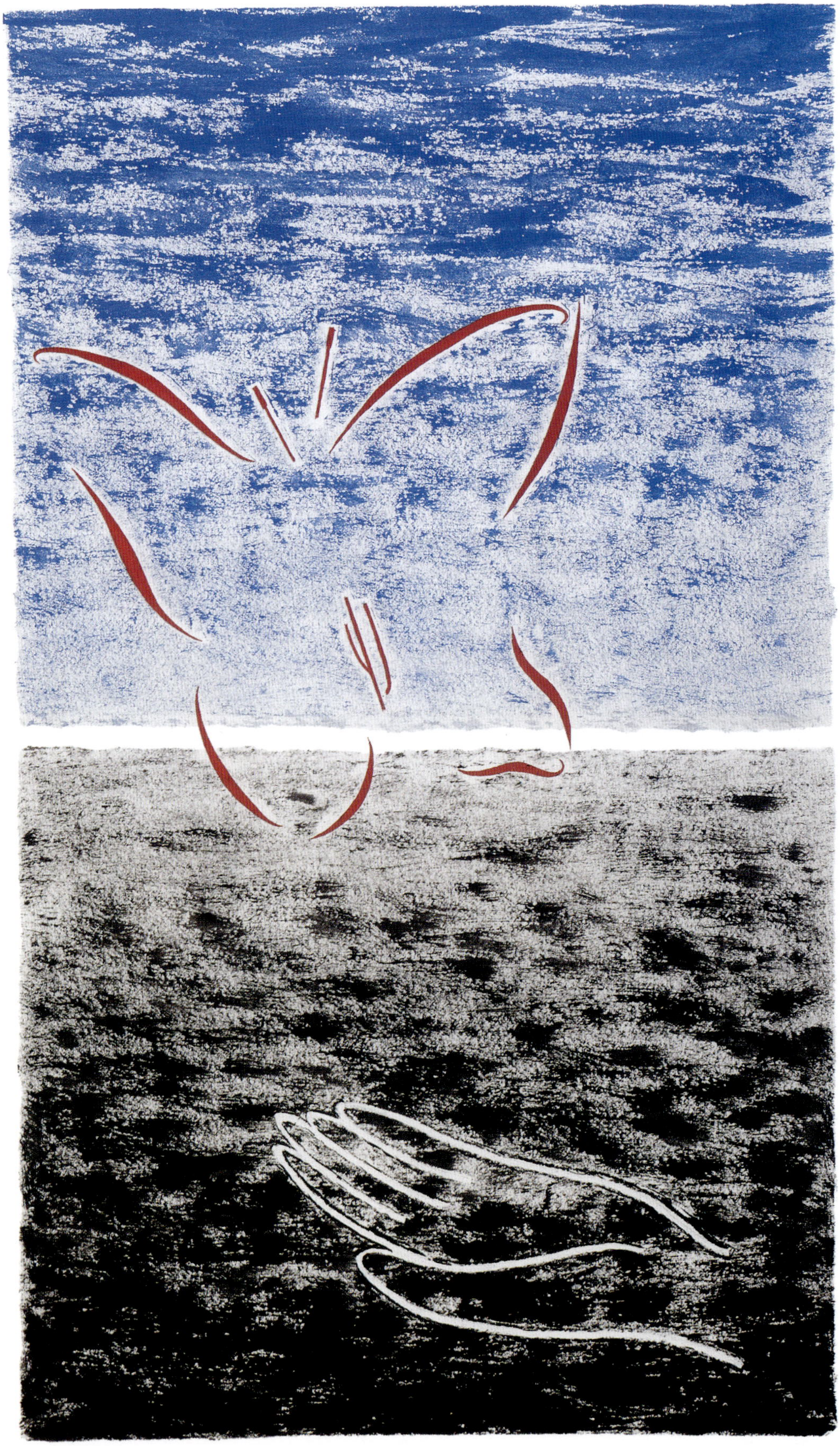

The Metamorphosis to Freedom

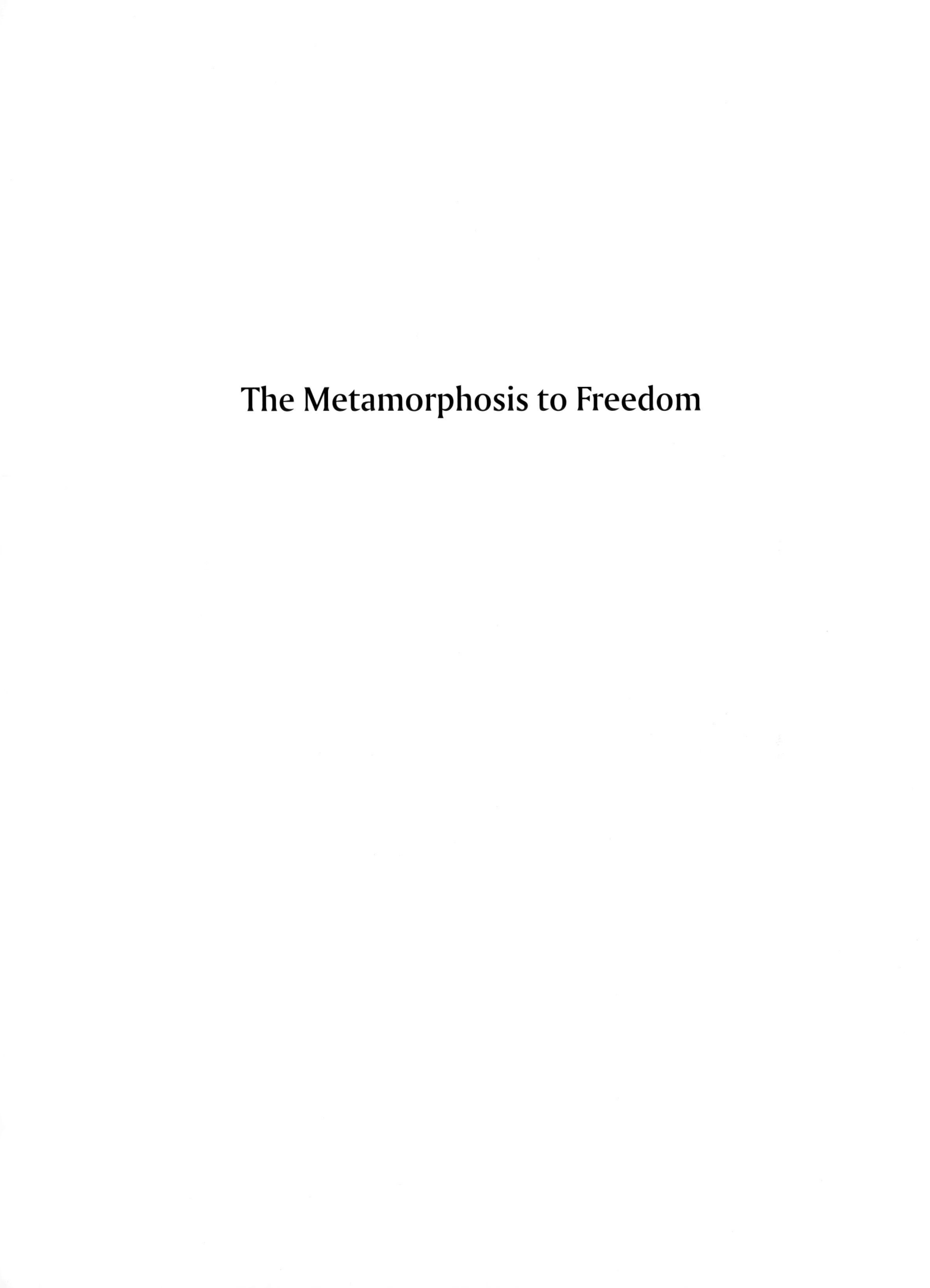

My Youth in Budapest

The Threat to Freedom

I was born in Budapest, the beautiful capital of Hungary. The Danube River separates the hilly side, Buda, from the flat side, Pest. I lived in Pest, in a yellow building. From my window I could see the Danube and, across the river, the Gellért mountain and the statue on its summit.

My parents worked hard—more than 12 hours a day on weekdays and several hours on Sundays. I was expected to study diligently and to respect others and their way of life, including their religion. My family was Jewish. Because my parents worked such long hours, I had a nanny, Anna, a devout Catholic who was a second mother to me. We lived in mutual respect with others. I enjoyed life very much. I liked to play, to draw, to laugh. I loved colors and music and flowers. I had nice clothes, good food, many friends and love.

Jewish people had been banned from military and government offices long before I was born. Jews could not own land, and they could not sell wine or tobacco. Scientific institutions were closed to us. Only a limited number of Jews were accepted at universities.

New laws in 1942 limited Jews in even more ways. Factories were required to discharge their Jewish employees, and young Jewish men were sent to labor camps rather than conscripted into military service. Membership in professional organizations (for doctors and lawyers, for example) was limited; only 20 percent could be Jewish. Marriage between Jews and non-Jews was prohibited. Failure to obey meant immediate punishment. Finally, Jews could not manage or own a business. As a result all Jewish-owned businesses—including that of my parents—were taken over by non-Jews.

Things got much worse when the Nazis occupied Hungary in 1944. Jews had to wear a four-inch yellow star on our shirts or jackets when we left our homes. Our cars, radios and jewelry were confiscated. We were not allowed to travel or to visit public amusement places. Our shopping time was limited. Then our homes were taken away. Every day thousands of people were sent to the Nazi extermination camp at Auschwitz, and for those who remained the ghetto of Budapest was established.

Dying in a bomb explosion was not the worst thing that could happen to the people in the Budapest ghetto. The greatest fear was that the doorbell would ring and someone would be taken away. We knew that we would never see that person again. This happened to my father, who starved to death in a Nazi camp. Anna's family hid my mother from the Nazis; my brother was at school in Switzerland. All my other relatives were exterminated.

In a Nazi Concentration Camp

The Loss of More than Freedom

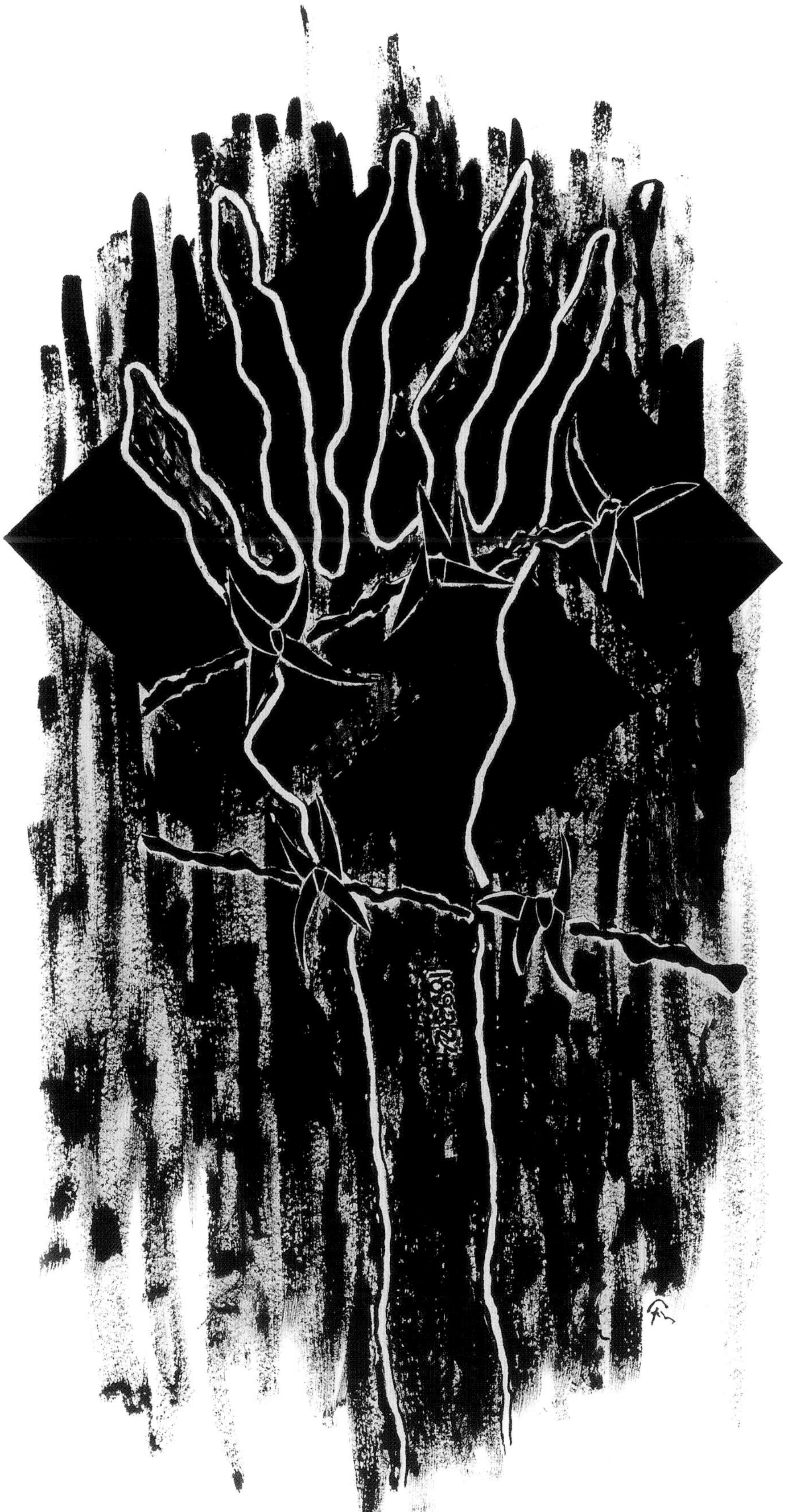

T HE NAZIS' GOAL WAS TO EXTERMINATE THE JEWS. They tortured and killed Jewish men, women, children—even babies.

When I was 19 years old, I was a prisoner in the Nazi camp at Gunskirchen in Austria. Gunskirchen was a death camp; it had no purpose other than to kill prisoners. More than 17,000 people—mostly Hungarians, like me—had arrived there after a 20-day march across Austria. Because we had barely any food and water on the march, we grew progressively weaker and less able to walk. The weakest were put on pallets rigged to horses. When the prisoners became exhausted, they were thrown directly into open graves, then shot.

Before I came to Gunskirchen, I had been in a camp at Mauthausen, also in Austria. I was at Mauthausen only four days, but it seemed much longer. It had been built to house criminals, but eventually anyone who disagreed with the Nazi government was regarded as a criminal. Over the main door was this message: "Work makes you free." That depends, of course, on who you're working for. I probably don't need to mention that there were no toilet facilities.

At the camp's dreaded stone mine, thousands of people died from carrying heavy boulders on their shoulders up the 186 "death steps". Many of the malnourished and exhausted prisoners were shot, or they were crushed to death by falling stones. Others were simply pushed off the steep edge of the quarry. Entire groups of Dutch and Hungarian Jews were killed that way. At Mauthausen I learned that it took 20 agonizing minutes for a person to suffocate in the gas chamber. Mass murders were carried out not only by shooting and gassing but also in less "merciful" ways, such as pouring cold water on naked victims and watching them freeze in the winter.

More than 100,000 men, women, and children from everywhere in Europe—and some British and American prisoners of war as well—were killed there.

A few months before I arrived, two thousand Russians had managed to escape. The Nazis hunted down and killed all but eight . To escape over the electrified 10-foot-high barbed wire wall, they had to disarm the tower guard, turn off the electricity and climb over the wall and wire. And then, weak from extreme malnourishment, they had to jump down. By then, most of them could not go any farther. The sirens were screaming, the SS guards from inside and outside the camp closed in with dogs and machine guns. Only a very few prisoners reached the edge of village. SS guards repeatedly searched every house in the village from basement to attic to see if any prisoners were hidden there. Family members were terrified. The guards killed every member of every household that helped the prisoners and piled their bodies in the village square. But some brave families succeeded in saving eight Russians. They were among the true unknown heroes of the war.

During my death march, sometimes a farmer or villager would run out with a glass of water for us. What a blessing that was! I wondered: what I would have done if I had lived close to where—day after day, month after month—thousands of people were walking in front of my house hungry and thirsty. Even if there had been plenty of food and no risk (neither of which was the case), how often or how long would I (or anyone) have tried to help? A woman once threw some apples to us. The Nazis shot her on the spot.

These people risked their freedom and their lives to help people whose freedom and, eventually, lives were stolen by the Nazis. Would you risk your life to help a hungry person under such circumstances?

By the end of the war, I had been a prisoner for months. When the American soldiers found me I was too weak to climb a single stair. I had to crawl toward freedom.

Communism in Hungary

Freedom Postponed

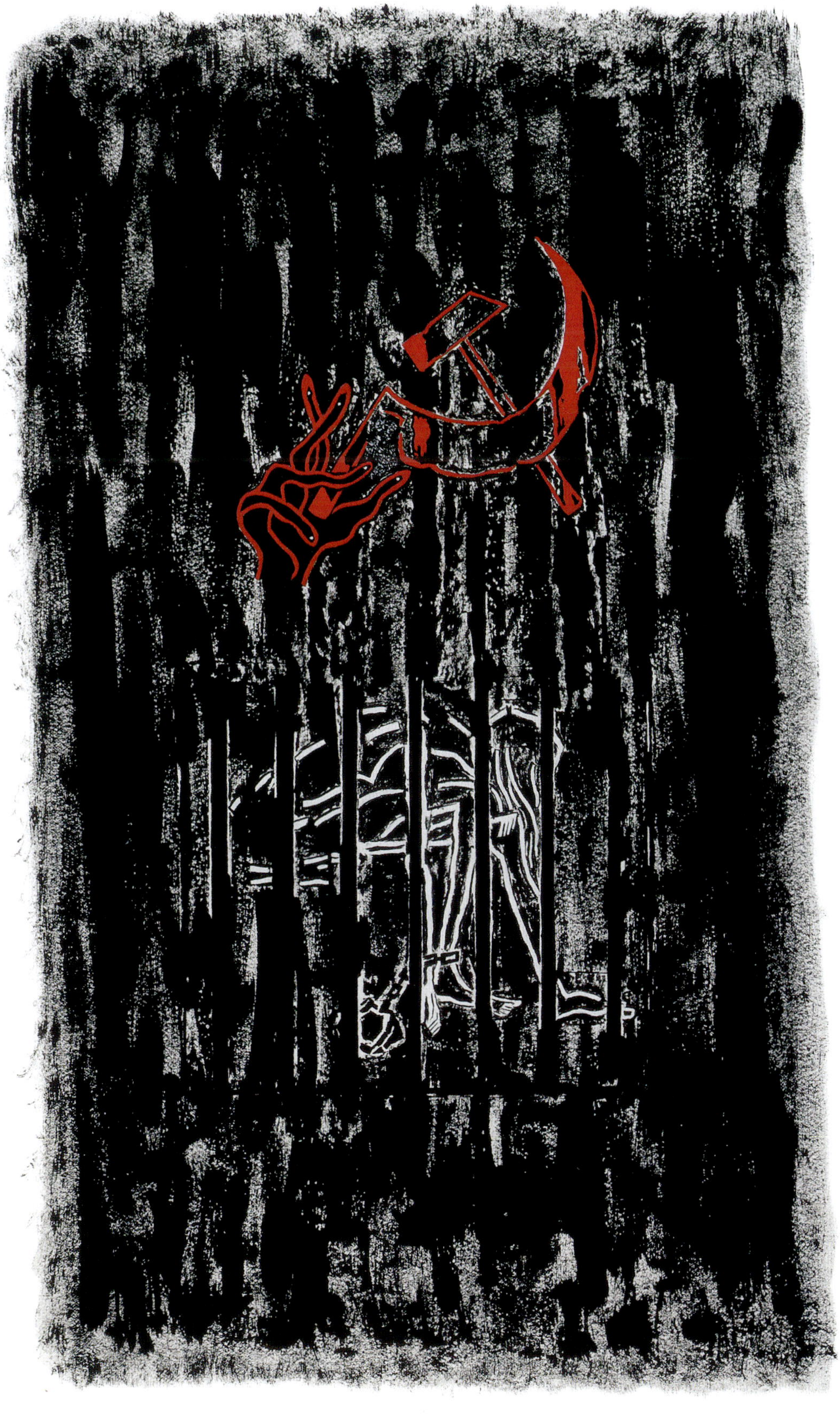

W̲HEN I RETURNED HOME TO BUDAPEST AFTER THE WAR, destruction was everywhere and it was not restricted to buildings. People and families were also in ruins. Gradually everyone started a new way of life.

Hungary—along with the rest of Eastern Europe—was designated by the Allies, who defeated the Nazis, to be temporarily managed by Russia. Instead the Communist took over industry, land and private property. Personal freedom was not to be restored.

At the beginning, a few large industries were nationalized. I felt that if companies could be taken away from their owners, if the rights of even a single individual were denied, then no one's rights were secure. Eventually our home and business were confiscated.

I was asked to join the ruling party. If I did, then positions, opportunities and doors would open to me. I had no difficulty in saying no, with all the consequences and difficulties of that decision. I could not become a participant in a repressive system.

Like the Nazis, the Russians had a secret police force, the KGB. Which was worse? Does it matter whether you are killed by a Communist or a Nazi bullet?

The harm from the physical and emotional insults of an SS officer or a KGB secret policeman is the same.

Tyranny is like dust: you don't see it at first, and then you notice that it is everywhere. It blinds your eyes, kills your mind, suffocates your soul. It distorts meaning and undermines public and personal life. It makes you afraid everywhere, even among your loved ones. It is like a poison gradually infiltrating your body; there is no hope and no escape. Everyone is ruled by fear, suspicion and distrust. Thieves and murderers are rewarded, and liars spread the gospel of hate.

At the beginning of each school year, pages of the history textbooks were torn out; what was taught the previous year was no longer suitable. We used to say that if the Communists said something, then even the opposite was not true.

I entered medical school in 1945, hoping to specialize in ophthalmology. Because I opposed the Communist regime, I was condemned as an enemy, and I was not allowed to be a specialist. When I finished medical school in 1951, I had to work out in the country as a general practitioner. A few years later, in 1956, with the help of some friends, I started to work in a hospital for premature infants in Budapest.

Revolution in Hungary

The Fight for Freedom

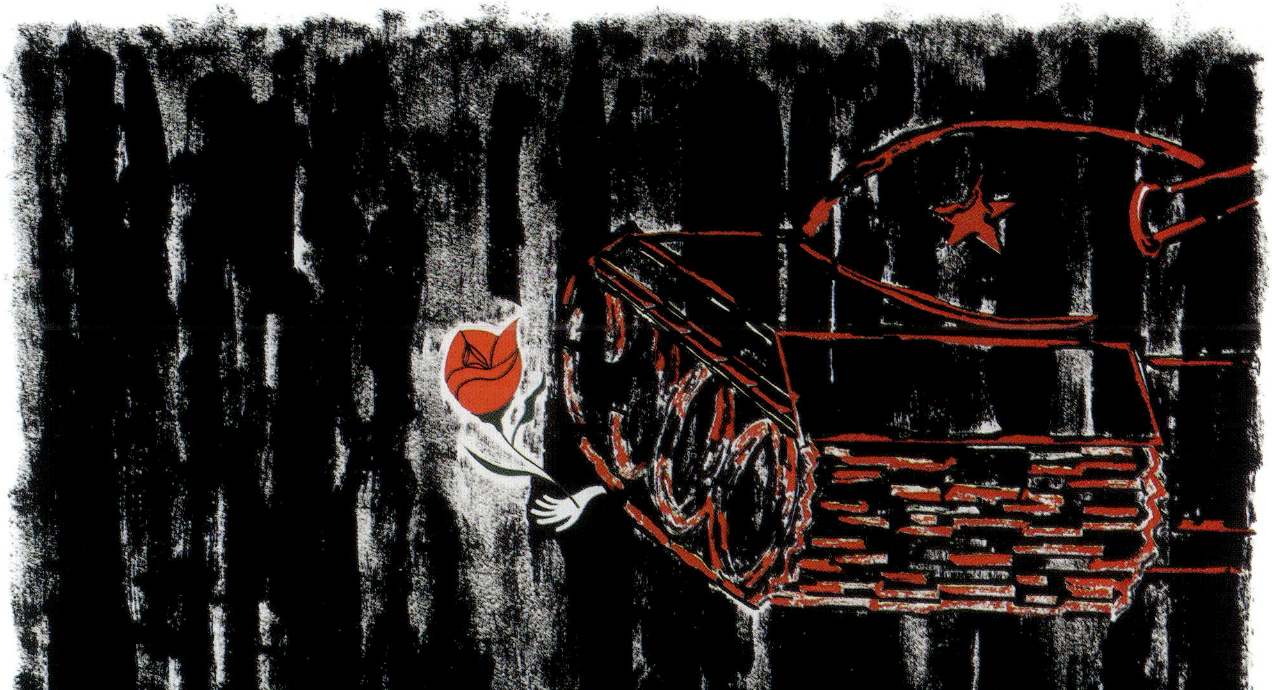

WE OFTEN THINK OF A REVOLUTION AS A PLAN carried out by a well organized group. But the Hungarian Revolution against the Communists was not like that at all.

On the evening of October 23, 1956, a cheerful crowd of students gathered in Budapest in front of the main radio station. The prime minister was supposed to arrive for a speech and the students hoped to block his entrance. The radio station was located on a small, narrow street. Because of the unusually large number of demonstrating students, additional secret police units were on hand. The students were actually cheering them, unaware of their ominous intent. I was attending a medical meeting close by, but I was more fascinated by this gathering than by the meeting. So I joined the crowd.

The students were as noisy as students everywhere, without any means other than their bodies to block the entrance. In Hungary at that time, only the police and military could own a weapon. At eight o'clock, from the balcony of the radio station, the secret police fired machine guns into the crowd.

My first thought was, what kind of government shoots unarmed students? My second was to interrupt the medical meeting and ask my fellow doctors to help the injured students. We took them to nearby emergency clinics. The street fell silent; the uninjured took cover and waited.

I went home. The next morning when I looked out my window, I saw children—some as young as twelve—with guns. The secret police had asked the Hungarian army for help, but the Hungarian soldiers joined with the demonstrators and gave them weapons. A revolution had been started spontaneously by students with the assistance of young soldiers.

This astonishing episode was the first obvious crack in the massive wall of a system that devoured entire nations, imprisoned over 100 million people behind the Iron Curtain, and for decades threatened the security of the rest of the world. The revolutionaries were young people searching for freedom, something they had never experienced before.

Some of my colleagues and I decided to help. With the assistance of other medical students, we broke into a government garage and confiscated cars to transport the wounded. Our volunteer rescuers, many of whom were killed, drove wherever there was fighting to pick up anyone who was injured—Hungarian and Russian alike.

In the hospital the freedom fighters discovered that some of their fellow patients were their Communist opponents. I convinced them that in the hospital we had only one rule: to help the injured. If they recovered, what went on outside was another issue.

Three 60-ton Russian tanks shook the buildings on a narrow street. A single small open truck followed with three youths atop it waving handguns and chasing the monstrous enemy. Usually tanks are powerful. But in a city, if someone risks jumping onto a tank to throw a Molotov cocktail, it becomes vulnerable and helpless. You just need courage, and the young Hungarian freedom fighters had it.

A Russian tank division came across the Danube from Buda to Pest. Teenage schoolgirls held hands in a chain as they stood and waited for the tanks to come off the bridge. The leading tank stopped, the top opened, and a Russian officer rose up.

"What are you doing here?" he asked the girls.
"What are you doing here?" they replied.
"We came to fight against the fascists!" the Russian declared.
"No, you came to fight against us," the girls answered.
"Who are you fighting against?" asked the Russian.
"Against the secret police."

The Russians joined the students and fought on the side of the revolution.

But idealism did not last long. Criminals started to emerge from the jails. Western outcries did not amount to much, and President Eisenhower reassured the Russians that he had no intention of interfering. I do not think they needed too much encouragement. Budapest was surrounded by heavy cannons, and Russian airplanes bombarded the city and the rebels. The world stood by. The United Nations held a meeting.

I was threatened with losing my job if I did not go back to the hospital for premature babies. Ultimately, I walked across the border into Austria with no intention of returning.

Two hundred thousand Hungarians took refuge in the West in the last months of 1956. Twelve thousand had died fighting for freedom. All the Communist parties in Western Europe disengaged themselves from the centralized influence of the Russians, and the people on both sides of the Iron Curtain realized that the invulnerability of the Soviet Union was a myth. The Hungarian Revolution opened the door for German, Czech, and Polish uprisings. It was the first break in the iron grasp of the Communist system, which was finally to disintegrate three decades later.

My Arrival in the United States

The Journey to Freedom

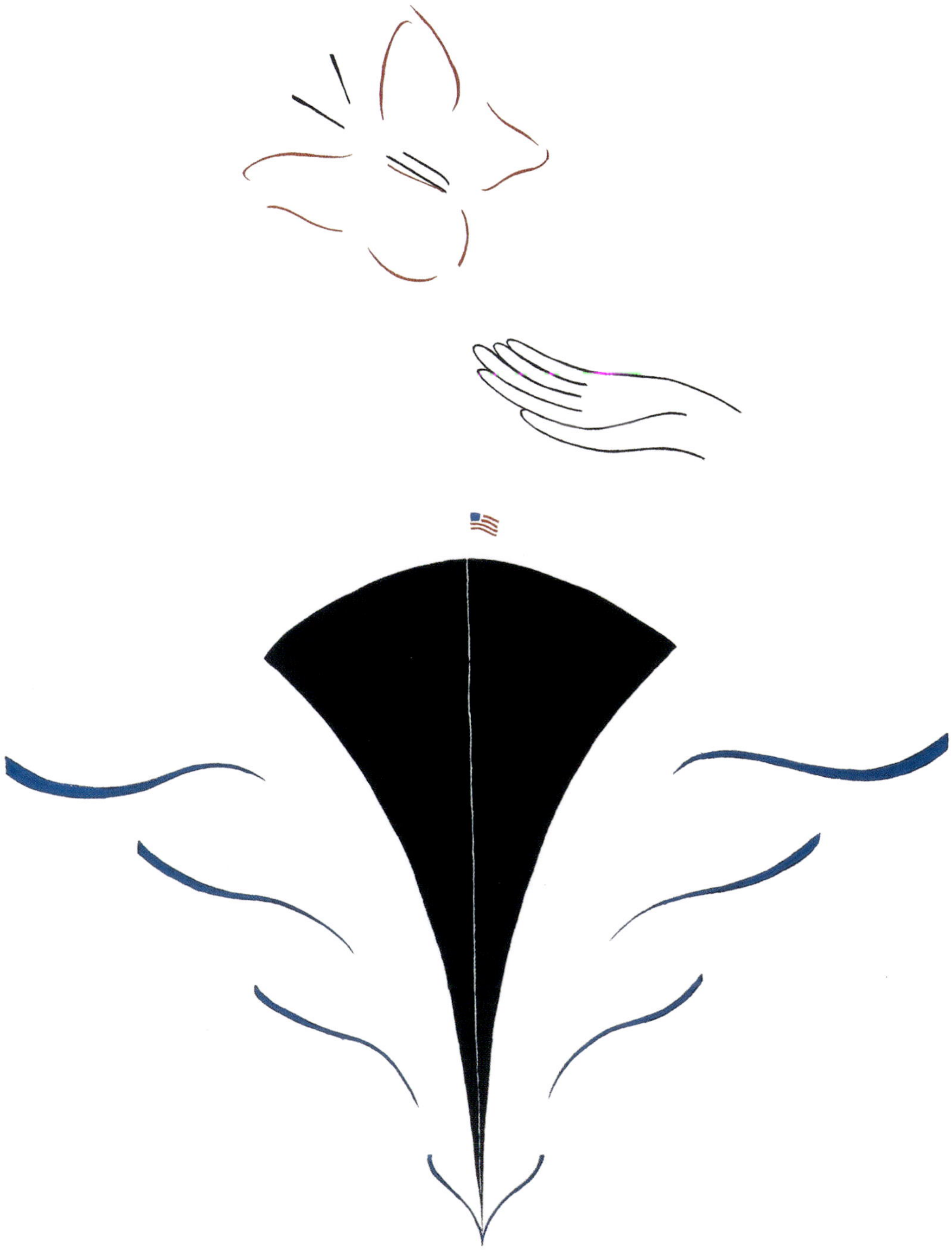

December 21, 1956. Bremerhaven, Germany. A U.S. Navy transport ship, the *General Eltinger*, was in the harbor with 1,764 Hungarians aboard.

I was greeted by a rabbi from Buffalo, New York. He said, "Please tell me, Doctor, I ordered kosher food for 100; will that be enough?" "I hope so," I answered. "I am the only Jew on board!"

The ship left two days later, and we ran into the biggest storm of the century on the Atlantic Ocean. Within three days there were only eight of us in the dining room; the rest were sick. I was so happy to be going to America. I even loved the ketchup!

The only hitch was that I had to pray morning and evening. As the only passenger who acknowledged being a Jew, I was the rabbi's only customer. The priests and ministers joined us for Friday evening service. My fellow Hungarians enviously watched me drinking Mogen David wine; they thought I might be getting other fringe benefits as well. Within a few days, others began to admit that they were Jewish, too, which relieved me from my daily praying routine.

At dawn on January 1, 1957, we arrived in New York harbor.

The day I came to America was the beginning of a new year for all and a new life for me.

American Citizenship

Becoming Free

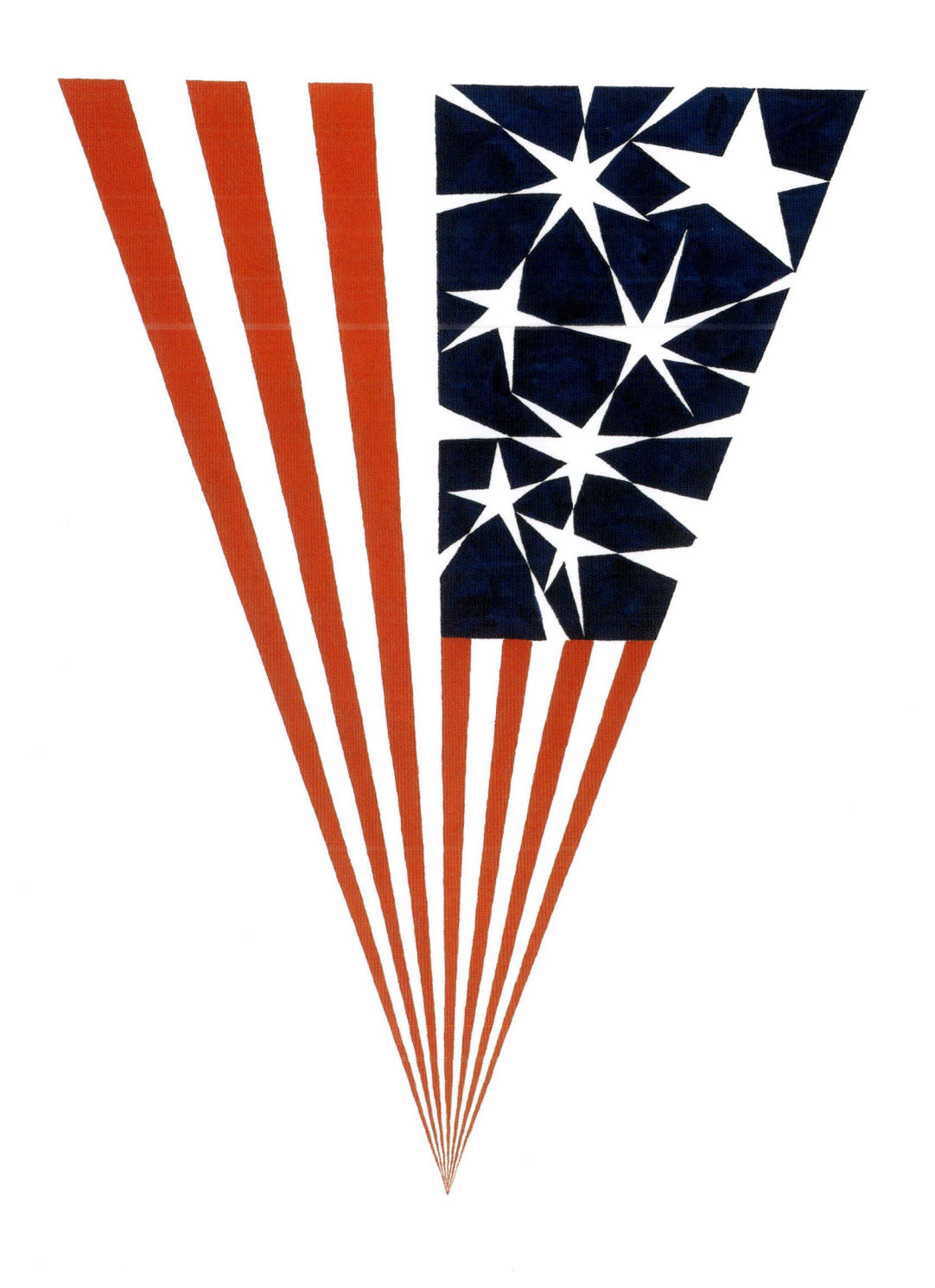

Rogers High School
MEDIA CENTER
Rogers, MN 55374

When I became an American citizen in 1963 at a ceremony in St. Paul, I spoke to a hundred other new citizens about freedom and opportunity.

"Not everyone had my reasons for coming to the United States. But even though our reasons were different, our conclusions are the same: all of us have decided that the United States offers us the greatest opportunities for success.

None of us was born here. None of us can take the rights and privileges of American citizenship for granted. All of us know that these rights and privileges will endure only if we accept certain obligations and duties.

Since I am a doctor, I often express my thoughts in medical terms. The addition of new citizens is like a blood transfusion for this country.

Now begins a new period in our lives that we hope will lead to happiness and satisfaction. Sometimes we will experience hardships because of our background. Citizenship does not erase old habits and customs. Yet it is precisely our backgrounds and our sometimes colorful, sometimes sad experiences that enrich us and others in our new environment. Whenever you are melancholy remembering the past, also remember that you left your old home, not because you disliked the streets, bridges, mountains and lakes but because you could not find the opportunities you desired there. Perhaps you were even afraid to express your thoughts.

Sometimes you may be homesick as you remember your ties to the people, customs and language of your country.

With the benefit of our past experiences and promise of our current opportunities, we will be able create a way of life based on our principles and our abilities. We will build a future for ourselves, our children and our communities by making valuable contributions—by giving instead of taking, by helping instead of depending on help.

What our future will be like, we do not know. Whatever happens, I hope we will be able to look back and say that it has been worth our while to become citizens of this wonderful country, that we have done our work to the best of our ability, and that we would do it over again. And I wish for all of us that our children will be grateful for our decision to settle here".

I shall never forget the day I received my American passport. I jumped for joy, like a child. I even kissed it. Becoming an American citizen was a childhood dream that I did not fulfill until I was 38 years old. My American passport and my certificate of naturalization are the most important documents of my life.

My passport opened doors and borders that always had been closed to me. I went places I could neither visit nor leave before. I was the same person I had always been, but now I was admitted and welcomed—merely because I was an American citizen.

A New Life

Savoring Freedom

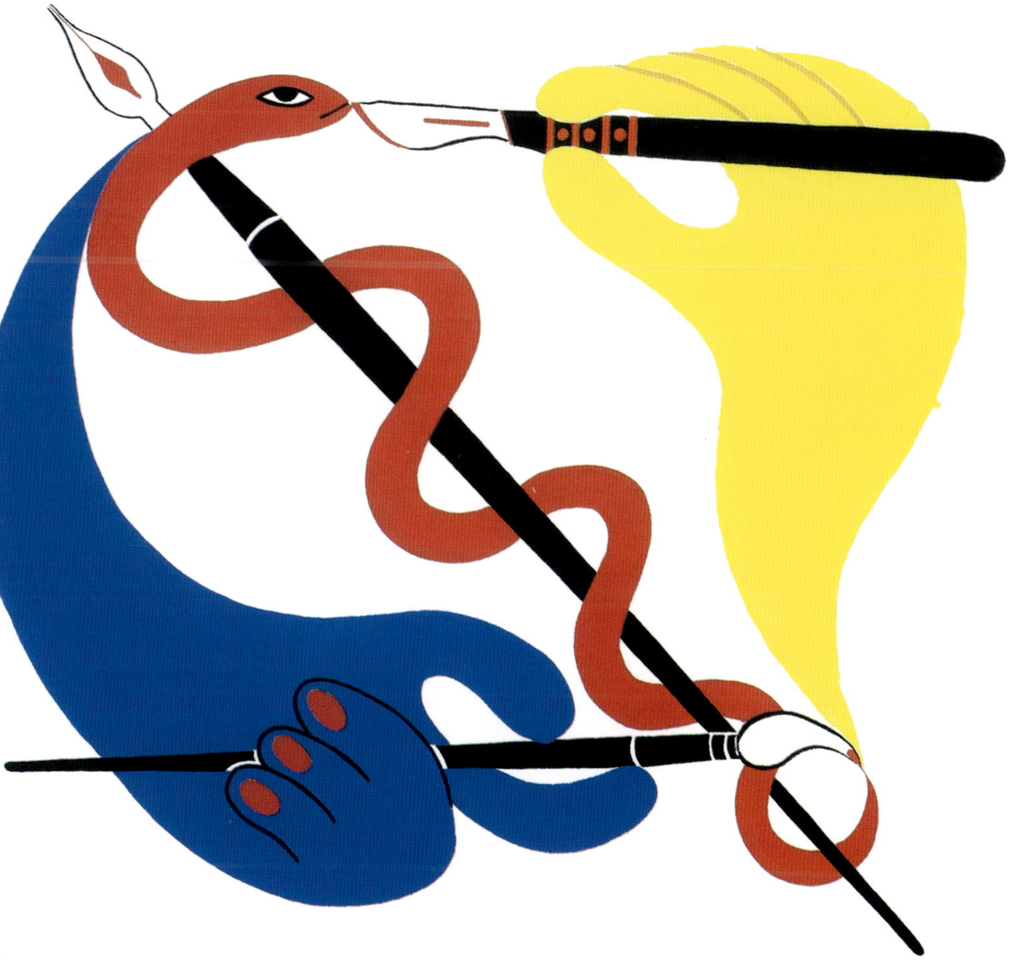

I ARRIVED IN MINNEAPOLIS FROM NEW YORK in 1958 to join the medical faculty at the University of Minnesota. Living is an art, and medicine is an art that makes life a little better and a little longer. Art and medicine are two consequences of the same desire to sustain life.

As a doctor in Hungary I worked with premature babies. In the United States, I became a pediatrician and a specialist in phenylketonuria (PKU), an inherited metabolic disease. In the past babies with this defect became severely retarded. Then a German doctor discovered that a special diet helped to prevent mental retardation.

Thirty-six years ago, a doctor at the University of Minnesota pediatric clinic was treating families afflicted with PKU, some with more than one profoundly retarded child. When he left Minnesota, he asked me to follow his patients. It was very hard on me. After we learned about the diet used in Germany, we prescribed it for a beautiful seventeen-month-old child with blue eyes and blond hair. When his mother put him down, he was like a limp rag. He collapsed and was unable to sit, and of course he could not talk. Two weeks after he started the diet, he was walking and began to talk. It was indeed a medical miracle!

Now doctors all over the world use a simple method to test all newborn infants for the disease. Our clinic at the University of Minnesota treats hundreds of families, and more than half of my patients with PKU graduate from high school and enter college. The most gratifying experience in my professional life has been to see hundreds of magnificent children who otherwise would have lived a meager existence, growing, laughing, playing, working, loving, receiving and giving.

I have only one daughter, but I have more than a hundred families!

During my internship I met a little girl at the University hospital. When I arrived at her bedside to take a blood sample, tears flowed down her cheeks in fear of pain. With curly blond hair and large amethyst eyes, she looked like an angel, but her face was covered with bruises, the signs of her disease. In her eyes I saw the tiredness and sorrow of a person who has been sick for a long time.

When we doctors reach the end of our medical resources, we feel a mixture of frustration and powerlessness. We search for answers that our knowledge fails to provide, and then we helplessly confront the inevitable.

We became friends. She began to serve as my English interpreter during morning rounds with the patients. When evening came and everyone had left, I sat at her bedside holding her left hand (her right arm had been amputated) and we told each other stories about our homes and cried together.

I told her about Budapest—the hills of Buda and the flat Pest—divided by the Danube River, which I always saw through my window. I told her about the thermal waters beneath the city, which has the only zoo in the world where the hippopotamus can have offspring. I told her about the Gypsies, wandering from place to place telling fortunes from cards and palms and playing the violin so beautifully, although they never had a lesson. The city I loved and had to leave.

She told me about her family's farm, the dogs and ponies, her grandfather (who, like me, talked "funny"), sister, daddy and mommy; school, games and toys. Above all, she talked about Christmas—the tree, the dresses, the songs and the colorful gift-wrapped boxes. Her exquisite face radiated joy as memory momentarily defeated her suffering. Then her tears fell like snowflakes as she thought of the beloved farm that was so far away.

There was no cure for her; transfusions just prolonged her agony. Her only desire was to be in her beloved home. Her parents and I agreed that she should have this wish. She went home, where death freed her from pain and suffering.

Fifty Years Later

A Free Man Visits the Past

1945

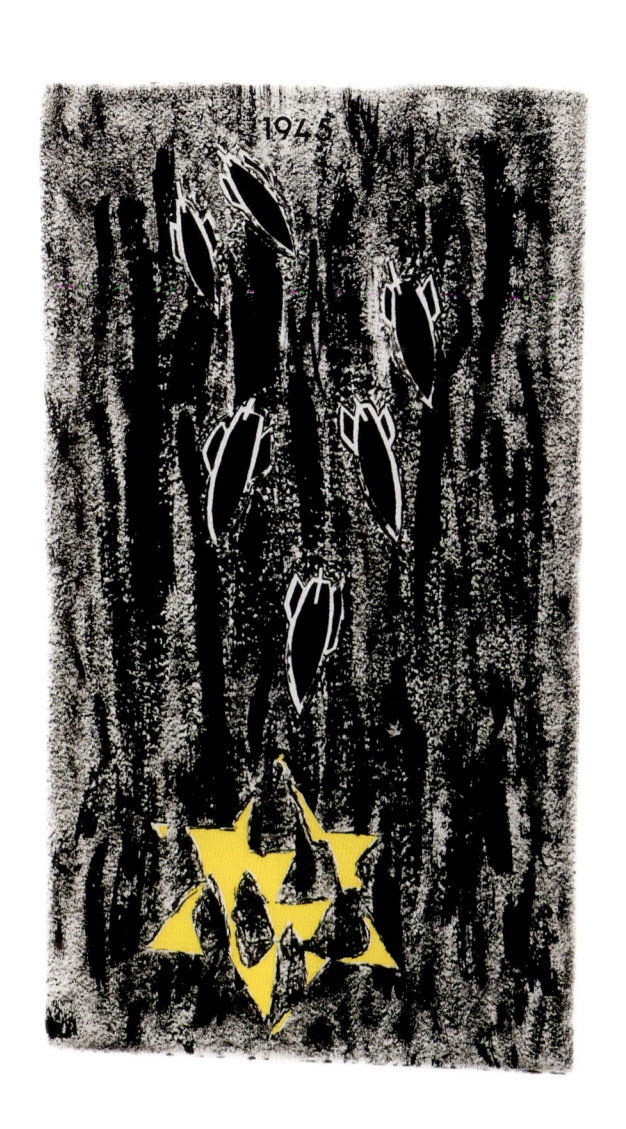

1995

In 1995 I received an invitation to attend the fiftieth-anniversary celebration of the liberation of the Nazi concentration camp at Gunskirchen, where I had been imprisoned. Some of us survivors as well as some members of the 71st Infantry Division of the U.S. Third Army would be there. It would give me an opportunity to thank the American soldiers for saving my life.

I arrived in Austria, slept in a comfortable hotel, ate a good breakfast and went by car with some others to the site of the camp, in the middle of the woods. The sun was shining, and there were newly grown trees.

It was quite different from my first arrival there. The woods now seemed peaceful. I felt nothing special; there was nothing reminiscent of the horrifying past. Temporary markers showed us where the barracks had been. I met Dale Speckman, who was a private in the American Army in 1945 and, accidentally, the first liberator to reach us. Speckman had been lost in the forest when he noticed a terrible smell—the smell of excrement and dead bodies, which led him to the camp and to my rescue.

Speckman now placed a yellow star wreath at this innocent-looking site, which was the last place on earth for thousands of people.

Back in the town of Gunskirchen, a woman in an audience of survivors, liberators and Austrian students stood up, held up a picture and asked in three languages—English, German, and Hungarian—whether anyone recognized the man in the photo. She was still searching for her father 50 years later, still hoping that someone might remember him.

When my turn came to speak, I addressed my talk primarily to the children of the town. I pointed out that even in the worst circumstances, there were people who tried to help us. At first, my hatred of the Germans was simple: "I will kill them all!" But when as a newly liberated man I encountered my first German, I had to make a choice. He was dirty and hungry, begging for food. I asked myself whether I should do to him what the Nazis had done to us. I gave him some food.

The high school students sang Hebrew songs and performed Israeli folk dances. Each of the liberated survivors sat at a table with a group of students, with whom we talked openly like friends. The students expressed their sorrow and stated their desire to live in harmony with others.

The next day at Mauthausen I saw the president of Austria lay a wreath on a memorial inscribed with these words: "May the living learn from the fate of the dead."

The people of the United States made enormous, unselfish sacrifices during World War II—not for themselves, but for others. The world should always remember and be grateful, as I am.

A Lesson of Love

———

Treasuring Freedom

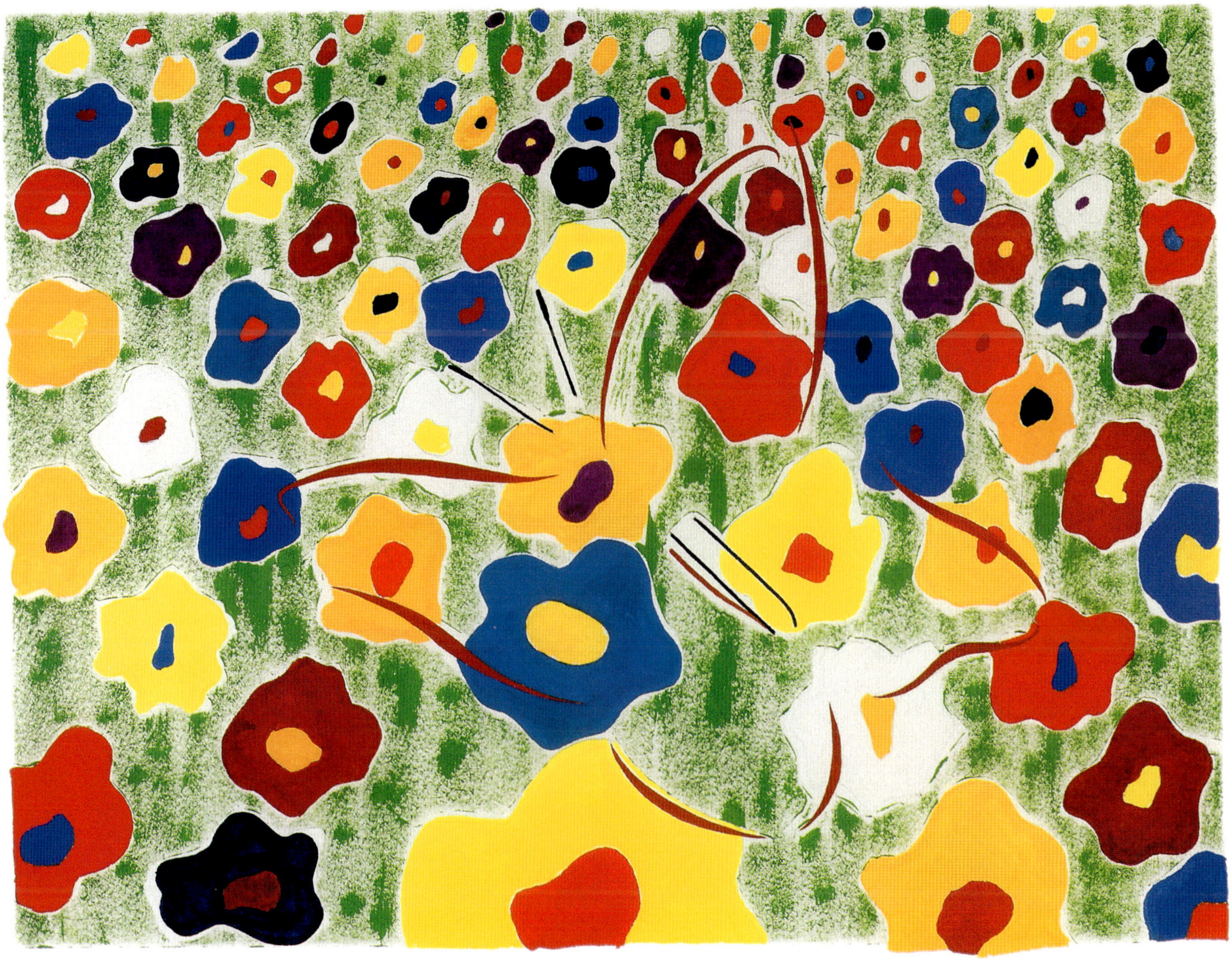

I AM A PAINTER AS WELL AS A DOCTOR, and in 1989 I was asked to illustrate the cover of a magazine and to write about my experiences in the Nazi death camp. My aim was to not to tell what had happened to me, but to express how I felt about losing my beloved father and others, and to speculate on what we can learn from the Holocaust.

The impact of my article was astonishing. My many Nordic colleagues at the University hugged me and cried—certainly unusual behavior for Scandinavians, who are usually so reserved. News of the article reached the local newspapers, and soon afterward I received an invitation to talk to students in Pine City, Minnesota. That invitation changed my life.

I find it difficult to talk to American young people about such a distant and painful subject as the Holocaust. And I am astonished by their positive response and curiosity. How would I have responded, at young age, if a strange witness from another continent had told me a nearly unbelievable story of such brutal atrocities?

In my lecture I pointed out that only one nation—Denmark—stood up firmly against the occupying Nazis and helped Jews escape by smuggling them out of the country. After I had finished and there had been some discussion, I turned to a student who had been watching me intently and asked, "Is there something you would like to say?" She stood up and said, "I am a visiting Danish student. My grandmother saved a family. Now I have learned how important it was".

The magazine article eventually led to an exhibition of my paintings and to a book entitled *Light from the Yellow Star: A Lesson of Love from the Holocaust.*

Having been a participant in the most organized, systematic extermination of any religious group in the history of mankind does not make me a reliable historian of that time. I am unable—and unwilling—to recall the horrors of those days. What I want to remember is not the horror, but those who stood up against oppression and sacrificed their own lives in order to help others.

If we do not stand up against a tyrant, we become either his victim or his ally.

Epilogue

The Lesson of Freedom

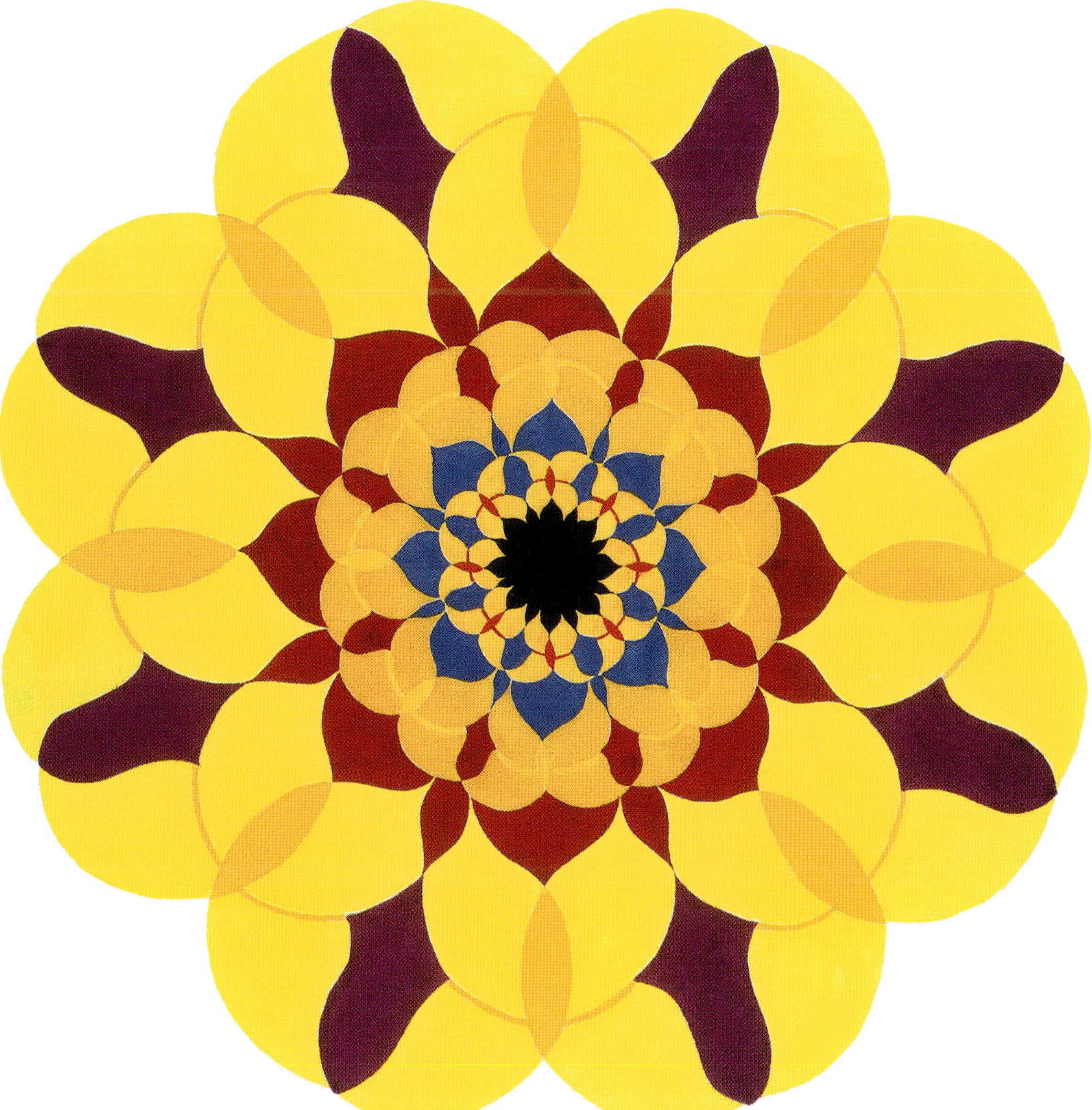

Regardless of who we are, or when and where we are born, we all go through the same life cycle: birth, growth, maturity, aging and death. Although we are individuals, we have more similarities than differences. We experience joy and sadness, health and sickness, strength and weakness, success and failure. We are all subject to the same physical and biological laws.

Our abilities may be different, but all of us deserve the opportunity to fulfill our potential. No system of government has given more people more opportunity to do this than democracy.

A double standard—one set of rules for this person or group, another set for that one—is always damaging in the end. Whoever benefits, benefits only temporarily. The Nazis sent me to a concentration camp because I was Jewish. After I was freed by American soldiers, I had to decide what to do when I encountered one of my former enemies, a starving man. One injustice cannot be corrected by another, so I gave him food.

We're all here together for a short time on a small planet. We all play a role in each others' lives. We all represent individual segments of a wheel. It may look like my part of the wheel goes up when yours goes down, but the wheel is really just turning toward your future and mine.

Think of yourself as a thread in a colorful carpet. Without the thread, there is no carpet, and without the carpet, the thread has no function. In the same way, your existence is meaningless without others.

To ensure a good life for all of us, we all must follow basic rules of compassion, equality and fair play:

- Treat others as you want them to treat you.
- Learn to understand and accept—and even enjoy—what makes us different.
- Join with others to guarantee freedom for all.

The most important lesson I have learned in my life is this: We must always remain human, toward everyone, in all circumstances, however brutal.

Like a butterfly breaking free from the darkness to seek the light, humans throughout history have sought freedom. Even those who have never experienced freedom yearn for it. Those who have it couldn't live without it. To achieve true freedom requires development, like the metamorphosis of a caterpillar into a butterfly.

We who are fortunate to have freedom must accept the responsibility to guard it and extend it to those who are less fortunate.

The Hungarian poet Sándor Petőfi wrote:

> *Freedom and Love*
> *these I require above all.*
> *For love, I would give up my life,*
> *for freedom, I would give up my love.*